AT THE BOTTOM OF THE SKY

DATE DUE

GAYLORD | | | PRINTED IN U.S.A.

AT THE BOTTOM OF THE SKY

POEMS BY

DONALD MORRILL

Mid-List Press
Minneapolis

FIRST SERIES: POETRY

Mid-List Press, 4324 12th Avenue South, Minneapolis, MN 55407-3218

Library of Congress Cataloging-in-Publication
Morrill, Donald, 1955 –
At the bottom of the sky : poems / by Donald Morrill.
    p.   cm.
    "First series — poetry."
    ISBN 0-922811-36-9 (pbk. : alk. paper)
    I. Title
  PS3563.08737A88   1998
  811'.54—dc21   98–16341
                                    CIP

Some of the poems in this collection first appeared in the following publications:
Ascent: "Grief," "Underprivileged"; *American Literary Review:* "Interview with Echo"; *The Chattahoochee Review:* "The Ascent"; *Cimarron Review:* "For the Old Rider at the Mall in Sioux Falls," "Betrothal Park: Iowa"; *Cutbank:* "Sentient Being"; *The Dominion Review:* "Sea Legs"; *The Florida Review:* "Back to Normal"; *Great Stream Review:* "Delicate Arch"; *The Greensboro Review:* "Singles' Guide to Marrieds"; *Gulf Coast:* "The Old Mentor's Reply"; *Gulf Stream Magazine:* "Ungrounded," "Among the Sirenians," "A Plateful of Hummingbird Tongues"; *G. W. Review:* "A Candle"; *Habersham Review:* "Nightly Constitutional"; *Hawaii Pacific Review:* "What Happens Next Happens Quickly," "Poste Restante: A Letter from Des Moines to Katmandu," "In Sichuan Province"; *High Plains Literary Review:* "Little Anodynes," "Ichetucknee," "Fairgrounds," "Produce"; *The Kenyon Review:* "The Feast"; *Laurel Review:* "Father and Son and," "Porcelain So Fine You Can Read Script Through It"; *The Midwest Quarterly:* "Elegy"; *New England Review and Bread Loaf Quarterly:* "For the Holidays," "The Hair Wreath"; *New England Review (Middlebury Series):* "The Taken: A Letter"; *New Mexico Humanities Review:* "Stewardess"; *New Virginia Review:* "To My Father's First Wife, the Adulteress," "Five Privacies," "Wherewithal," "Junket"; *The North American Review:* "Onus"; *North Carolina Humanities:* "The Boy Who Would Go No Lower in Price"; *The Plum Review:* "Profile," "Another's Old Diary, Just Opened"; *Poet Lore:* "Thunder in Sunshine," "Last Photograph of His Bachelor Hand," "Travels of Rusticiano of Pisa"; *Prairie Schooner:* "Bejeweled"; *Quilt:* "Milk Dump"; *The Reaper:* "The Hiroshima Maidens"; *The Southern Review:* "Blue Star Home."

The epigraph is reprinted from *The Nature Observer's Handbook* © 1987 by John Brainerd with permission from The Globe Pequot Press, Old Saybrook, CT, 800-243-0495, www.globe-pequot.com.

Printed in the United States of America.

ACKNOWLEDGMENTS

I would like to thank the Virginia Center for the Creative Arts, the Dana Foundation, and the Arts Council of Hillsborough County, Florida, for providing support that allowed some of these poems to be written. I would also like to thank the teachers and intimates who have given me good guidance and encouragement over the years. Finally, I would like to thank Lisa Birnbaum, Richard Chess, and Alane Rollings for their invaluable help.

Contents

Most of us spend our lives at the bottom of the sky, aware of air when it is too hot or cold, too wet or dry, too windy or too breathless for comfort.

—The Nature Observer's Handbook

Ungrounded

*You know, I'd see those refugees every night on television, but I didn't
really believe they existed until I became one.*

—*A man forced to live in a tent city after
Hurricane Andrew destroyed his house*

At any moment you pick,
lightning touches earth
in a hundred places.

Averages decree it.

At any moment you pick,
bombers bank on ultimatums.

One more degree North,
and it would have been you.

It would have been you.

• • •

In the Tiki Bar, the nine-fingered piano player improvises
for those who think the lost digit implies character
and mutilation, truth. His style accompanies the tourist longing
for the calm center of a swirling mai tai.

Lightning blinks like a blind eye on the horizon
and moves out to sea. The sails of the Thursday Club
crowd the distant inlet like teeth in a shark's mouth.
Everyone has to be from some place inescapable.

• • •

Among the tents,
a *Life's a Beach!* towel
hangs like a stage curtain.

Offerings fall into the case
of a wretched fiddler
almost pausing between phrases.

At any moment you pick,
averages decree it.

Through the rubble runs a street,
part of the order of a house
now strewn:

Cross it, a child was told,
and you're grounded forever.

• • •

The teach-in. The talk show. The demonstration.
The clean-up. The benefit. The black market.
Ghost towns will be taken and retaken.

Watching, how long before we bore ourselves
with suffering and the sighing cold-kettle faces
to which too many are entitled?

• • •

Don't tell a woman who still hears the big wind
about burning cities elsewhere
and invaders feasting on zoo animals.

Don't tell a man who grieves on the tidal surge
about a Fountain of Sacred War Martyrs
flowing red with food coloring.

Don't talk about history's ration queue
when night is coming again with the looters.
Not now. Not yet.

The Hiroshima Maidens
USA, 1970

I can't find the photograph of my father in Trinidad
with a beer in his hand and, on his shoulder, a monkey
wearing his sailor cap. It is lost, burned,
like the flash-whitened faces of these women
reassembled for this picture by the surgeon's gloved hand
years after the bomb dropped with peace for the Pacific theatre.
An overloaded circuit, bad insulation—they said that was the cause.
As our roof withdrew into its rafters, collapsing
onto trunks, old books, the uniform I'd folded to steal,
I thought of the cigarette I'd hidden in that place
crushed hurriedly by my mother's call to lunch.
We'd rebuild. But the next time he cut my hair
I sat still without those snapshots of him:
radioman second class, air corps, drafted before graduation.
The clippers buzzed my ears like fighter planes
as I recalled his glossies: the geisha painted on the fuselage,
the hatch he'd hung his legs out over empty, shining water.
My temples whitened. He dabbed the nicks,
telling how they trained him to float using only that cap,
and a drunken pilot nearly crashed him once
in the gulf between Americas. Now, these women,
some with the small, bored faces of their children, unmangled,
crowd this magazine far from home or what was home;
and everything seems clear, even the edge of shadow slicing a grin.
On leave in the jungle, he passed out in my favorite navy whites.
Sleeping with him on our living room floor,
I dreamed of his look toward his smoldering dream house,
the bombardier whose buddies vanished in their first flak.
I could smell the fumes from our upper story,
the reek stinging like the scorched hair of these women,
grown back, chopped uniformly short. From the fire and sickness
of radiation's half-lives, they are recovered—
these memories, our maidens, hopelessly retouched.

4

FOR THE OLD RIDER AT THE MALL IN SIOUX FALLS

I didn't have change for a jug of Thunderbird
when, drunk and busted by your old bulls,
you yelled, *Quicksand!*
I made you, sonofabitch,
kowtow! and had me by the arm, mumbled rodeo,
and hugged my neck as I tried to back away.
I kept smiling at passers-by,
but I must have looked like your boy,
come for the old man and used to the sour breath
of a life story trying to escape.
You clutched my collar like a strap
as I yanked out from under your dead weight.
And your grip minus two fingers was strong enough
to almost strip half of me
as you fell, face banging the tile,
and I dragged off toward the parking lot and home.
I knew then the world is full of drunks and people holding on,
and people stopping sometimes to imagine why.
But I ditched that ripped shirt in my neighbor's trash can,
my anger useless as a consolation prize.
Some gate opens when I feel those few seconds rustle,
barely harnessed by recall or fortune.
Then Quicksand, fevered, bucks riderless into flight,
and in the dirt those two pinched-off fingers lie
like a warning to let go or be thrown.
Whoever you are you may still be dying,
somewhere sprawling to the dust.
I can only guess, no longer anyone's boy
but in moments like this,
when suddenly you appear
and I am already wrenching away
half exposed to the future—
where every beast I dream
breaking you
is ours,
and the helpless thing lives, bruising, human.

BLUE STAR HOME

The blue star displayed in a house window means
knock on this door
if you're chased by a bully
or shadowed from school by a stranger in a car;
someone will answer,
will know what to do;
the world as you've felt it will remain so;
you're welcome,
don't forget.

But we do forget
even as we pound furiously for help,
or stroll past, imitating, on a plastic recorder,
a mourning dove.
Or living too deep in the back rooms,
out for the day,
we don't hear.
What was that?

When we answer
and discover that child in the frightened eyes
of a colleague, or our reflection,
we may bid it enter.
Before closing the door behind it, we peer out
for the threat,
for veracity (we've been tricked before,
we showing the star).
And there's our street. There's a maple leaf, fallen,
wide as a breastplate.

I wash dishes and talk in a low voice
to my ex-wife on the telephone, who's gone on
with things enough to miss me tonight
and believe it's eight years ago. I talk low
because the woman I love now
reads in the next room, trying not to listen
for some further clues to me. She likes clues,
believes they reaffirm the mystery
she wants to feel but can't, her current wisdom
making all fiascoes and evasive franknesses
an old spousal kiss. She's capacious in her recognitions,
and capacity seduces me like nothing else.
So I scrub and clink in the warm suds,
the receiver nestled on my shoulder
like a prom date for the slow dance.
I listen to the voice I once decided
I could die with, its casual evangelism,
a tone. It doesn't want me back but wants
to want me back. Its furnishings encroach, tonight,
and I'm still eager to pity it—time laughing at us,
time deserving our revenge. In my low voice,
I comfort and think of an old teacher
declaring all Minds *lumpers* or *splitters.*
In my hands, bubbles cluster, convert.

SHIM

On a street where walking
means you're crazy or for sale,

a man on foot waved
a white flag tied to a twig.

My surrendering side
still drives around his block,

part of the rush hour where
we grow up and try to live.

In these times, I hear a name
banished from a collegial mouth

and wonder, Is this us,
vagrants on judgment's stoop?

In crossed legs of seated officials,
I see heartbeats kicking slightly.

The sky then seems the same
horrid headline as last year, the mirror

a petition for change I've inspired
but refuse to sign. Once,

under a house propped on jack posts,
the boy who used to be Yours Truly

swam in dirt, his mother above him
on a ledge of grassy twilight,

magnanimous in her permission.
I remember that between

the floor joists and each post,
wood shims, cobbled on the spot,

helped to level up the house
poised for a new foundation.

A home in air. And a boy beneath,
refreshed and blackened

by his imagined ocean!
So simple to swim in our dirt, as dirt . . .

From that man waving his dead branch,
what answer would solve us?

The day floats like a house
needing a shim to be righted,

words, deeds, we offer—
sometimes gracefully—or withhold,

keeping things uneven,
to ourselves.

MAN AND RUG

He hangs it up for all to see, this life,
and begins to pound the past from it.
His footsteps and dreams, the heart traffic,
swirl out as dust that must go, that must.
Each season renews, doesn't it? And the self?
The man starting over beats out a time
untuned to his punishing cleanliness.
That pattern before him, that weave,
ravished his eye when he could still think
such possessions *beauty* and replaceable.
He's behaving, this man, he is—
having paid and unwilling to pay again.
This flying machine, these stains,
this body whipping itself toward a purpose.

Pardon Nong An.
Now that it's reopened
by the central authorities,
its dust tans the few
who will come. Its pagoda with bells
jangles on the breeze
and that's all. Pardon
the boy staring at the stranger
in the public toilet. He, too, wants to see
if distant peoples are the same.
The girls with legs whitened
not by hose but scratches
will change faster than shelves
bearing the twelve new consumables.
Magazines creep in.
Someone sneaks away,
so that horseshoe print
in summer asphalt
glitters in a dream roaming
without proper documents.
Pardon the old,
who've only had each other
for decades. No one can shout "hello"
at an outsider, to impress a girlfriend.
Not yet. Most walk fields
without looking down,
strides measured by furrows.
Pardon Nong An,
so pitifully inner, its hope
expanding with the restaurant menu,
its interest in cameras
and suspicion of new policies.
Now that it's reopened
it can pardon you.

(China, 1986)

FAIRGROUNDS

No suspicions of deeper inclinations
rush the boys with water and gunnysack,
deciding who will pour into the hole
and who will bag the frantic, furious ground squirrel
if it chooses the same burrow exit.

As usual, the grandstand is empty.
They haven't had to snip and sneak through
the chain link topped with barbed wire.
When they must, later, stirred by memory's
motorized carnival and industrial show,
they'll see the cut close up behind them,
this green before them in all their plainness.

By then, they may be partners in the firm.
One may be dead. One may have moved away
repeatedly, hungry, from childhood,
for houses where the candy dish sat full,
untouched, and the voices remained quiet.

They'll have heard the tale of dud fireworks
that maimed another not far from here.
They'll have come to know us, as we know them,
by the eyes which flee, or willfully stay—
the quick choices which flush us out,
captives we can't keep alive
and are frightened to release.

AMONG THE SIRENIANS
FLORIDA, 1890S

Large aquatic mammals of the order SIRENIA; surviving Sirenians are
the Dugong and the Manatee.

The steamboat out of sight,
Thursby and Son haul up the sugar barrel
nudged overboard by a sleepy crewman,
spread the crystalline clumps on the dock
to dry, they hope, before ants take the larger share.
"It's a little sweet gift of the river," brown
like the brackish main channel
that brought the family through lily pad and cypress knee
from Unemployment, New York.
In the house perched on the grassy mound
flecked with snail shells left by Seminoles,
the morning's pies cool in the locked cabinet—bartered cherries—
and the Mrs. dusts the fainting couch and the *Haywain*,
makes up the younger son's bed tented by the fine, white netting
he's pulled down clawing back from nightmares.
The Miss, downstairs, wipes the "lynx window,"
through which the night once leaped
onto piano strings.
It's locked, even in summer, now.
Beyond the pane's slow sag in the frame, beyond cabbage palms
and the footbridge, the boy turns
from the spring into which he's dived again
hoping to reach its dark source.
These waters fresh to the surface, clear, nearly airless
but flowing toward life,
draw him along the shore
toward the *blue talapia*
sucking and spitting gravel from nests on the stream bottom,
and toward something unfamiliar,
huge, white like clouds but more still,

something taking air from his world to another:
six slow clouds
which nibble the floating flowers.
Books will tell him they come inland from the sea
for warmth in winter, that sailors thought them mermaids
and Indians, gods,
that man is their only enemy.
But now he watches them
and the alligators nearby imitating logs, always.
Who to cry out to?
Of the house, he can see only the lightning rod
and the catch tank that turns rain into running water.
At the confluence, his tiny father
slaps his brother on the back.

At Casa Feliz

When I put my mouth on your second mouth
in the true dark of island night, I remembered
the dinner guests near the wall of jasmine
so fragrant, that once, they could hardly taste.
My eyes widened more than on the blanched day
I first went down on the world and stared up,
trying to command a look back of extra pleasure,
gratitude. "Unimproved" is what the city calls that
darkness we found ourselves in—meaning,
only, no lights but stars along the roads.
Your plush stiffenings, your signal breathing
named it *close.* How many assumptions
we've set our lips to! How many people
we had to lose to get to each other . . .
That morning, shellers claimed their best treasures
come after storms. I want no part of shells.
I tried to glide my tongue like the ray's wings
near warm, pearling surf—our moans for god
throttled so as not to wake our hosts.

TO MY FATHER'S FIRST WIFE, THE ADULTERESS

In the bedroom where your ecstatic cry
died against dusk-veined windowshades,
I later slept—as they had slept who made me
after my father caught you there
and cast you into whatever memory,
whatever dream he would try to forget.
He kept the place and built on
with each addition to our family,
mixing new lumber with seasoned stock
from houses wrecked for an interstate.
I pulled the old nails, and he hammered;
and we could tell a piece of heartwood:
hard to take or let go. Yet I knew nothing—
as it seemed my mother knew nothing
when I finally came to ask
Why marriage? Why him? hoping for a word
about the me who'd called her *Stump!*
and snatched up my hammer on the way out,
so soon becoming like him. She said
I love you only in reply.
The day I first heard your name
I was a boy who saw betrayal
in having tickled his father's feet once
and that man waking furious with laughter.
Since then, I've heard some call you
Freedom, Exile, even Fate,
and have wondered at the glitter
of a sheared common, and what your cry was for.
When you telephoned that one time
I was told to take no message,
and they shared that, they who called you She.

Goodbye, she said, for good.
And he stood there in the tub, shivering
after she shut the door softly,
too softly,
sure it would open again with her return.
And in the long soak thereafter, he began to realize
such waiting is the way religions are born,
their necessary terror
always personal.
He thought of her dying elsewhere,
and he repeated her harshest words,
now hearing the need lodged between them.
At times, he could smell her particular odor.

And he cried, of course, cheap tears,
then those that burn the cheeks.
Enlargement, awareness—
there were many imperatives, many resolves.
A pine cone fell on the roof.
The cat bawled at the window for food.
Though he'd never clutched a whip or leveled a forest,
he understood, later,
that it was not love or hope he desired—
there in the womb-water
growing cool, shriveling his fingertips—
but mastery.

Was it birth he chose then,
seeing light scar the page of his journal
and leave it blank?
Was anything like that a choice?
Sometimes he stared at her empty closet,
as if to remember her happy or sad.

Is this what they'd tried to hide in each other,
the passing? Now he had this moment
like the acorn in his palm—
the tree, the branches, the leaves falling,
curling into smoke.
He squeezed hard, harder,
then mercifully stopped.

Another's Old Diary, Just Opened

It may compare the spirit to dooryard fruit,
the gnat which flew into an eye and perished;
may house the boys napping, with erections,
before the TV, and a ripped parachute.

Sun may descend the throat of a glass swan,
a red glove bud in a snow fort in spring
among the many pages of unexamined life
ancient as euphemism. Each phenomenon—

like a mounted deer head—has its background.
Grandfather's posture imbues a floor lamp.
The platoon is made to stick out its tongues
to reveal who ate the forbidden horehound.

How petite this world is! How accurate
its hammerings! Sight (in-, fore- and hind-)
was pulled along these passages in a rickshaw,
toward some judgment undeciphered yet.

Through monumental clouds and recipes for glue,
one bit of dialogue that tasted real,
we, the expected intruders, make our way
toward what there was, and is, and how they knew.

IN SICHUAN PROVINCE

In midwinter markets,
you will find stacked, ruddy as leathers,
hog faces,
peeled from skulls
and pressed flat.

Though they smile with a heavenly primness,
brains boiled
and served on platters elsewhere,
though they seem to keep a cultic secret,
or wish to beguile
state inspectors,

one winces slightly,
as if embarrassed in solitude;

a furrowed brow
makes another look judicious;

and there's the scar on one
frightened by a wheelbarrow.

Oh, these sacrificed kings
laced through the snout!
These masks of appetite!

They know what we've come to expect
of them and ourselves
and conform enough
to make festival broths,
dangling from purchasers' arms!

(1986)

MILK DUMP

Husbands emptied canisters
into the frozen, hacked-out trench.
Wives shook placards at news cameras:
Boost Dairy Prices!
Later, snow puckered at the windowsill,
and Aunt Eva hummed, smelling faintly of cigar,
as she poured warmed oil into my sore ear.
A lullaby, and the black earth unfolds,
and the dreamfrost uncurdles,
the refilled trench
a grave until plowing.
Owl-eyed in bed,
I heard with my untended ear
the sleeping house
and the next dawn, pails,
in the valley,
catching.

Produce

At the market, a man slips two bananas
into the pocket of his worn fatigue jacket.
He stares at us, three nearby shoppers
clutching carts equipped with calculators.

We stare off intently, pretending to our lists.
So he holds up another banana—
like a chemist examining the vial
of the newest miracle cure—
then slides it grandly into his pocket,
grins at us, and strolls toward frozen food.

Later at the check-out, he's next to me,
paying for bread and milk and one TV dinner,
watching what I'll do without the two strangers
who allowed me to ignore his theft.

I still wonder why this accusation
captures the listless outlaw within me,
and why I think that outlaw a failure.
My collaborator, he watches with some knowledge
of how the fruit of our meanings is picked,
lingering for me to turn him into something.

Then he's off, turning at the automatic doors
as they bag my purchase and this week's promotion
(volume nine of *World Book Encyclopedia*);
and he pulls the pockets of his jacket inside out.

JUNKET

:For which the town is turned out to wave to us,
  and the peppers are polished and the marketplace pretending,
  and the department shepherds panic and give chase
  with a dogged courtesy—getting themselves lost—
  when we veer into any dirty and darned side street.

:On which we are bussed to the Ya Lu River—for five minutes—
  and to the ginseng factory—for three hours!—
  and served tepid cola before the ziggurat
  where girls in white chiffon gowns beckon
  for us to join them disco-dancing,
  to show how it is done where we come from.

:Through which—excepting banquet toasts and drunken singing—
  we avert our faces from the Ministry's cameras,
  while still getting to visit this restricted area,
  transported by private train, no less.

:After which, like the clearest of consciences,
  the day out the window going home
  presents bare butt boys near laundering rocks,
  leafy twigs wound around a peasant's head;
  and one thinks of silk paintings bound up as sacks for pillage
  and that this thought is another collaboration.

:After which the night conductor lowers green velveteen;
  and one ties it back to watch the hardsleeper bunks,
  reflected in the glass, dreaming over the land,
  and smokes quietly with one of the shepherds
  almost relaxed, happy for the ride, such as it is—
  one who suddenly draws from the dimness between us
  a wishbone too fresh to break.

(China)

23

NIGHTLY CONSTITUTIONAL

At the Roadway Inn in Melbourne, Florida,
the northern old emerge from their rooms
to circumambulate the parking lot at evening.
In twos and threes, sometimes solitary,
sometimes exercising their capacity for news,
they drift outward to the perimeter of pavement,
strolling clockwise through the empty spaces.
What do they see, pausing to note weeds beyond?—
miles from a beach, from children's children
whose drawings decorate their poolside windows.
Surely they've heard the chewing sound in leaves underfoot
and point to something else besides those orange trees,
the windfalls, another lug of suns.
Surely they know the life bending not to break?
Others can afford a better view, perhaps.
These promenade this edge until the dogwood blooms,
until surf shops and balconies teem with northern young—
these with fallen branches lodged in other branches,
flourishing in their one season.

He agrees that no man is an island
and works to keep his islands free from man.
They lie six miles from the city center,
three breeding grounds of beach and mangrove
on P.R. loan from a conglomerate.
He says "our population," meaning birds—
cormorants, white ibis, royal terns—
and knows, by last count, how many pairs of each
nest there, more familiar than is usual
with a wing or two of flocking nature.
The three game wardens killed by plume hunters
when plumes were worth two times their weight in gold
invest his gaze like ancestral prophets.
He's a seer of *nonprofits*, who's overseen
the predatory raccoon's banishment,
who burns shore brush preventively, and rototills,
and slogs through meetings with directing boards.
Once he might have strapped himself to smokestacks,
to beg the broadcast eye of evening news,
or sugared dozer gas tanks, spiked tree trunks
destined for the clear-cut harvest—except
his revolution comes from inside out.
He sets his time bomb in a rack of slides,
its fuse: the talks his shyness makes a trial.
He says "our population," meaning us—
the audience and all that nest beyond—
part of a graph that's never flown so high
without plummeting. He knows that wildness
isn't going to help itself enough;
we can't flee that like bored listeners flee him.
All's tangled like the feathered corpses found
on a line of cast-off monofilament.
What arrogance in trying to save a world
and make a living! Almost metrically,

almost sacredly, he talks and takes donations;
he plants the plugs of marsh grass in a row,
spaced evenly as on a vain, bald pate—
hoping they grow thick together, weaving
as they become themselves, like a new mind,
and hold the sand against its own erosion.

Porcelain So Fine You Can Read Script Through It

Sandy, from next door, walked into the kitchen
and found my mother holding a soup bowl
to the gush from cracks in the aquarium.
The hammer my sister swung into the glass
as she yelled, *I'm outta here!*
still lay on the linoleum. My mother stepped over it
as she stretched for another bowl,
which Sandy handed her.
                              My sister knew my mother
would save the goldfish before opposing her departure.
Sandy told me later my mother looked relieved
to have the goldfish to rescue. When the aquarium almost emptied,
she helped my mother transfer the nearly-doomed
to the bowls—to the familiar, poorly-filtered water
of a new dimension.
                              My sister has been gone for years.
She's stopped following her carnival man.
She rents in a neighboring suburb.
And the house in which Sandy burned in her sleep
was bulldozed. Its vanishing exposed my mother's kitchen
to more direct sunshine.
                              In this light,
my mother taught me the box step,
leading, as always, by following.
She backed away and pulled me toward her,
and smiled as I glanced up from our feet.
Just step through me, she sang, *like this . . .*

SMUDGE

Going out bareheaded into this first decent spring day,
I was stopped by dawn angling through a window. It lit
a large smear from the greasy rag used to clean the pane—
a smudge that looked like a swirling Chinese dragon.
In China, that creature is a god not to be slain,
if one prizes fertility. Through it, I saw purple cosmos
yet-to-bloom, blooming, sickled for the seed.
I felt the ocean that surrounds one wader's waist
and the healing wound itching to be opened. At that moment
a million migrating butterflies, each a monarch,
swarmed a dreamed drilling platform off the coast;
a pilgrim faced his life in a corner of a remote train station, crying.
I wondered what kind of advice *Just Be Yourself* is
when The Dipper of stars is also The Plough, also The Cart . . .
No sword to put this god to, I thought, or this version of self—
no time as the light moved and I hurried with it to meet you.

THE HAIR WREATH

Each paying half by agreement,
we saved it from the junkstore window:
blonde and auburn with a shock of brunette,
and spangled with paste-pearl daisies,
a Victorian braid of domestic madness,
tight, and thankfully not our fashion.
Now our bad taste makes it twice a relic.
It's another *us* undivided, forgotten
like a maverick mine in a once-strategic bay.
Did you pack it here "on purpose" or did I?
I used to die against such useless questions.
I lift it from the box now, careful of pins.
What boors we were! boring each other,
making that resolve not to go to bed angry.
And you, claiming all was desire and object,
my fear of your mind, sure as a stiff prick.
What does one say? We'd imagined
three dead sisters sitting nightly at vanities,
the hundred magic strokes from their brushes
curling in the casket with older locks;
and their three vested suitors
exchanging cards, whores' addresses,
chatting on empire at tea. Very clubbable.
We were hardly so vivid with ourselves.
You claimed all my touch was only token.
And, much later, we made a truce of the thought
of how much we are alike. Fingering the strands,
I see you rolling us a smoke, my best editor,
pointing to the dry patch on your back
you can't reach with oil. This wreath.
I've dismantled it a hundred times.

The Feast

I'd been stateside long enough
my lack of prospects
was making me look questionable,
yet not so long I couldn't sense the wealth in things here.
Even common bond paper had a weighty extravagance
I'd not felt before—
which allowed me to think, for a moment,
that I wasn't a part of it,
but more worldly somehow.

                     Mornings on the porch,
I'd roll a sheet into the typewriter
and watch my past
rise as résumé, remembering how once
such brazen credentials seemed
(according to a friend in college)
"pathetic supplications
to the gods of middle management."

                            Now, mulberries plumped
over the rotted shed,
and Meg and I talked
of making a pie—
to sweeten living
on her slim tips from that bar
run deliberately at a loss. We were waiting for ripeness
in sufficient numbers
before venturing out on the mushy roof to pick.

And maybe it was the bluejay swooping downward
through the levels
of the backyard—darting up
                     to perch next to another of its kind—
that put me in mind of the male huia bird
hammering a hole with his hard, blunt beak,
stepping aside, then,

so the female's tweezering bill
could gather their precious grubs
from deep in the tree.
But I thought of them—
mated for life, exquisitely dependent
and now extinct—
and was glad
that analogies, however adapted, proved nothing;
and winced, recalling
the first time she dressed for that job—the repulsion,
the fear
at how she looked like those trapped women
trying to get through,
ones you might leave extra change for,
if they were quick
and friendly.

I came to notice the bush shook
from within;
and one by one, its ripest fruits
vanished unaccountably,
or dropped into stains.
An office took me on.
And on a day free of it,
I saw in those purple splotches
the steps we hadn't taken (if we could have taken them at all),
steps we hadn't needed
this time—nearly forgotten
like the gauge of beseeching papers,
or distant desperation (say, a friend's)
reaching out
toward green berries.
For a moment, then,
the blue wing fed within me,

and I was richly laden. I could hear her coming,
with the bills and her law books,
up the stairs
toward our kiss
                        not sustained by two mouths only.

THE TAKEN: A LETTER

I stood among foot traffic
on the Puerta Del Sol,
singular and glum,
doubly outside. Then
a couple on a motorbike
parked not thirty feet away.
If beauty had meaning,
theirs declared them inseparable.
They embraced and kissed
as she was beginning to cry.
He looked up from her
as if for advice from the scene.
They were hands in hands,
like wrestlers.
                    Finally,
he smiled and rubbed away
some of her tears
with his left index finger,
tapped her lightly on the chin
and said something
that made her smile a moment.
As he turned her gently,
she pressed into his palm
a white handkerchief—
and crossed the street,
looking back once,
and was gone.
                    He stared
at impulse turned to cloth
there in his hand,
shook his head slightly
and rode off, trailing
a thin rope of blue smoke.
A moment later, she reappeared.

And stood where they'd parted,
the day roiling around her.

When Marco arrived,
he listened like the loan officer
he said he used to be,
and speculated that maybe
they'd tried parting in private,
and needed a new place,
one neutral at the start,
a place that would make them
quick.
      "Come," he said,
and we entered the cafe
where the night before
my daypack had been stolen
while we sat with the Freid sisters.

The man behind the counter
shook his head No,
said to me, in translation:
He'd seen no such article,
They kept no Lost and Found.
And turned for confirmation
from his wife at the meat slicer,
her nod that all inquiries were vain.

As we walked to some place different,
Marco told of two pistols
in New York Fast Food,
of lying face down with others
sharing imminent death,
the wristwatch in his shorts
gouging his abdomen.

"This watch," he said,
showing it like a brand.

Why they hadn't seen him
hide it as they robbed,
he didn't know.
They were junkies, yes.
"But some things," he said,
"are too obvious.
We wear glass blinders.
I didn't know what I'd done
until afterwards."
                    The watch
was a gift from a woman
who couldn't have known
if it had been taken;
it had been years then
since they'd talked—
                    "So logic
dictates," he said, smiling.
And apologized for ordering
our coffees *con leche*
without asking my preference.
"But these past three days," he said,
"you've had nothing else."

We sipped and wondered
about the woman of the watch,
he, it seemed, wincing within—
until he turned to ask
"Was the man who approached us
with flowers last night
the thief's partner,
the diversion?"

                    A daypack
with notes, an address book,
Love in the Time of Cholera,
a cheap Walkman with my voice,
tuned by white wine,
begging Don't Leave Me,
though it had already left you.

I like to think that tape
carries dance music now,
my erased words
somehow underneath,
the fencible part
of the personal.

There would the Goyas
at the Prado, and the Freids,
who turned out to be,
on second meeting,
mother and daughter.
There would be *tapas* and *cerveza,*
and Marco's reservations to China—
canceled by the student massacre.

We sat in just enough shade,
the few clouds sheer
like fine handkerchiefs,
the moment, as now, surrendering
more than could be accepted.

THE ASCENT

People we don't know
are unfolding their dreams,

spreading the silks,
upping the flame to a hiss.

Each rounds out slowly
into what fullness was meant for.

The first wobble and lift,
trailing guys and applause.

Those after are soundless,
the crowd who's come for beauty

quelled by repetition or wonder.
Numbers, logos blur above

each basket growing smaller,
deviled by higher breezes,

the life inside, waving back,
superseded by lighter designs,

planetary longings and the chase.
As dawn crests, it must compete

with a hundred spheres—
happiness

rising from nowhere
like bubbles in breakfast champagne.

Sea Legs

I

After the engines quit on take-off
and the fuel-heavy wings
somehow cleared the concrete jetty,
the fuselage nestled on the bay;

the rescued flight crew found itself
ordered back to the runway,
another craft—no time to brood—
the same mission, the same war.

Years later, the lucky pilot fishes
though he's seasick.
He hooks a snapper and lets it dangle
in the Gulf's green shallows.

He staggers to the berth below,
to rally his bored son topside
and, secretly, give him the surprise,
a good memory of something on the line.

I don't want to! howls the boy, at last.
And the pilot, woozier, ascends.
He stands, braced against the pitch and yaw.
The gleaming chop churns up in him

the shiny metal wreaths he tossed
upon that bay beyond the jetty,
five wreaths for the crew of the *Anxious Agnes*
sent up forever in a tropical depression.

Fixed on the horizon's steadiness,
he's surprised he needs to reel it in—
this silver flash of wing that anchors him
to the art of keeping what he must let go.

2

Now accustomed to The City, rarely grasping
as the subway car reels and jerks, the son
holds his daughter on the way to day care,
smiles at women old enough to miss their children,
young enough to offer him their seats.

RACE WAR! shouts a nearby tabloid,
pictures of a flaming skyline and the looter's glare.
He recalls his first day in this underworld,
the new "interview" suit that made him
feel wonderfully, uneasily, like Dad—

and the gray film on the inside of the paper cup
thrust under his nose like a gypsy's tambourine,
the cracked hand there demanding coins.
He'd stared ahead, fixed on some vanishing point,
ashamed of his absurdly gold cuff links;

and later on a 19th floor, amid expensive art,
he'd given answers that led him to this morning
scheduled around a nasty conference call.
He thinks of his father building thirty years of tires,
his angry *I remember* letter, their rapprochement.

A lurch, and his daughter tumbles into headlines
behind which sits a graying black man—who shakes off
"sorry." For the first time here, the son
sets his daughter down to stand—no thought yet—
and they sway, his hand clasping hers clasping his.

A Dust Devil

On the day you or I fix the boss's brow
with a wide, wet smooch—a double ear-yanker—
a dust devil will spin
up the long mahogany table, the spine of each manager.
Memos will swirl with the mad ruination:
Behold, one of your own is escaped
from the usual ambition!
The roof will levitate on stupefaction and secret worship,
the fool's sun lighten death
on every positioning face.
And you or I will walk out the door,
going we don't want to know where—
just away from those remaining
as the whirlwind abates and the carnival of unmasking
is veiled in group laughter,
the agendas resumed.
True, *away* is not so simple. The betrayer,
if not hammered to the ground or blacklisted,
is offered "advancement"—
his mouth, stuffed with money,
well mummified.
We sit with this world. The one to be kissed
recognizes himself in us.
This is our business among the pretenders
until the day you or I rise
to make a motion.

WHEREWITHAL

The demonstrators assembled
needs around a statue,
driving pigeons away.
Relatives from abroad—
dumbfounded by their wealth
in the Old Country's currency—
clutched peacock feathers
that had tickled their chins,
eyes hoping for some purchase.
One son in the cafe
stopped pounding his point
into the clouds
of marble table-top;
and another, resistance
long in his joints, rose
from thin-stemmed wine,
half-standing as he reached
to pull back the window curtain.

. . .

What time was it
as the trumpeter marked the hour
the Tartars invaded
for the twelfth time that day?—
his touch, in the steeple,
not as bluesy as the night man's,
the noted warning
again dying precisely
as the arrow pierces its throat.
State Radio then switched
to a little Chopin.
Two sunbathing by the railroad
didn't hear the chants

for Change. A mother
among scratch plows
rubbed gums cutting first teeth
until her fingertip, too, was numb . . .

                            • • •

When the regime at last sweats
like a cheese left out too long,
when the despot's bodyguard
laments in his memoirs
that he couldn't fetch
his fallen boss
back from despondency;
when the Opposition's paintbrushes
stiffen beside its rolled posters
only in a teacher's summary,
and the New Order hopes to last
as long as proverb,
who need remember, if possible,
the universe of purpose
that day pigeons circled?—
the girl with chocolate ice cream,
next to the poet's spattered bust,
lapping up the approach
of riot police,
the scrubbed-ham faces
TV Elsewhere hadn't sought yet,
still a napping Zeus . . .

                            • • •

Relentlessly, the day went on.
Imprudently, the stars persisted.
Just off the silenced square,
in a street of facades
where Copernicus studied motion,
ammunition from the water cannons
gathered and dispersed
peacefully between cobbles.

(Cracow, 1988)

FRUITION

Berries of spring
darkening my walk,
I have no time these days
to sweep you up—no leisure
to contemplate your fullness
robins didn't feast upon.
You crunch under my shoes
as I go out to meet my office work,
the handshakes with *attitude*
pinned to their lapels,
flip charts of my old enemies.
Not that I'm complaining.
When there was time to wonder at you,
I didn't, harried with my mirror.
And you know my foreignness
to brooms. What good
is regarding you? Distraction, that death,
has always been my silent partner.
I never thought to pick you
as I never thought of the fallen
ripened and left to rot. Now,
I hear the hardness of your seed,
a voice that may be poisonous
to us hungering for accomplishment.
I can pay to have you cleared.
Instead, you stain my soles,
leave a trace through the day
of all that should have gone
into a bird's belly, or a mind.

A Plateful of Hummingbird Tongues

Just beyond
the articulate,
at the edge of notice,
lie things we believe, now,
are most crucial.
The obvious
has everything
to hide,
because it conspires
to be simple,
and we are never simple enough
to see ourselves
in it. Consider
the king's special dish.
His idea
of imagination.
Or his advisor's,
who loves the power to suggest.
The first bite, no doubt,
goes to the court taster for poisons.
Does he savor armies
swinging nets like swords,
prismatic feathers
darkening ice in buckets,
flowers abandoned?
Some people think
this matters.
The throne room hovers
over questions
of extinction
and sustenance. And we,
unlikely to have such delicacies
named after us,
gaze at the guards

with their weapons,
and at the hoveled woods
receding from the window,
appalled and stilled
by the judging jaws' work.

Artificial

Nick twists the bolt in his prosthetic knee:
"Why did he do it!? Because the world's a lie—
artificial—people, that is. Dumb fuck . . .
And how could he do that when I get up
and put a smile on and *this*? It hurts, *this*.
It won't even go a sixteen-hour day
without breaking down. He was some friend, man . . ."
Not knowing the suicide in question,
only this poet whose health is helpless,
I sit, my silence growing false, and say,
"You can't do anything but live,
cancer or not. It's your strength. And not his."
"Yeah," Nick says, tapping his flesh-toned plastic,
"I hate it, and I need it. Some art, eh?"

GRIEF

Just gold,
and not 24-carat,
but it makes the winter golden.
A woman he's never met before says
Good to see you again.
A man at a bar pats his ass,
or is it his wallet?

At first he's not too surprised.
He's looking people in the eyes again.
Even his friends throw him a party.
But that night, his sorrow at her loss—
sorrow slowly withdrawn from public—
gets swept back further than he's planned,
to a privacy unprepared.

A little gold.
The next morning he fingers it, thinking
It's one of the softer elements,
easily reshaped to fit local needs.
And the body rarely rejects it.
He sees a thousand watches and rings.
He knows what he first meant by it.

Then spring comes,
the opening and closing of her jewelbox,
all he won't wear.
And he's happier.
A chameleon darts across the pavement.
And by the river, a woman kisses his other ear
as they argue about the cinema.

Gold. That summer
she mentions she doesn't like it,
that it's not *his* style.
But already he's imagined
the puncture closing up
into a tiny scar.
Nothing natural about it.

THUNDER IN SUNSHINE

August on the porch, sunlight on my closed eyelids.
Behind me, like a beast I've stumbled upon in nightmares,
a downpour growls, stalking inland from the sea.
I can't wake up. I'm trying to weigh the pillow
a man used to suffocate his brother,
by agreement, in the last long days of cancer.
How briefly must its underside have held
the contours of the drugged face, thirty-five,
and faces like it waiting in the family room.
I hardly know this man, my neighbor, yet I see him
through his wife's oblique confession to my wife
sit with that pillow in his lap, smoothing it,
just starting to be alone with his brother.
I imagine him trying to remember any moment
that could have brought the two of them there—
in childhood, say, when they mounted the spiny back
of a stegosaurus in a crude theme park,
and whipped its concrete flanks, riding away.
To be at home, that is what we say, wishing.
And this man who cares daily for his shrubs
rose, at last, from that bedside,
stepped through that room's threshold
sold soon by the new widow,
knowing what more about the end of pain
than when he had arrived?
                                  Now thunder prowls closer.
I feel the pillow underneath my head and wonder
how we dare sleep so soundly
when we can't wake up.
I want to ask his wife what promise she might fear
as he nuzzles her breasts in the night.
And what of those roses, over which I've shaken his hand,
and my wife, who earlier danced naked in the kitchen?
In his yard, a gold light shrouds the live oak
I've vowed, on simpler days, to emulate.
Its leaves blink at the first drops. Our fleeting fragrance: earth.

ELEGY

—for M.D. (1949-1991)

1

The stare of the bereaved, a peeled potato.
One child old enough to understand
one not. This evening,
the open microphone stands before the gathered.
Last night, it transported a sonata.
If you hear now,
hear our words,
not our thoughts
(which you would only know anyway as your own—
human, embarrassingly various).
Must we always be reminded,
this way,
to live?
A candle weeps in each hand
until there are no more tears, no more words.
Once, fishermen cast back into the sea
the crab with the carapace resembling a samurai's face
(reminding them, thus,
of an ancient, drowned boy-prince)—
a shell-face thereafter
borne more often to their nets.

2

Auras peel and fall everywhere
from things that moved you.
Still,
the live oak makes its simultaneous motions,
as before this city became its companion.

Somewhere, your image inspires,
perhaps good.
This is how it looks.
Forgive us
this bright morning
how long into your eternity?
Shade roves the properties.
You will let us go, please,
enough.
You, gone tomorrows
to which we dare not make comparisons.

Sentient Being

On tablerock in country that breaks a spade,
a campfire heats milky tea
and the circle of well-paid pariahs
sharpening their cutlery for dawn.

I approach this light, uninvited,
trailed by the far-off baying of monastery dogs,
more sure in darkness of the path than of motives.

Here, the foreman points with his fedora
to a boulder, a smashed camera—
the line not to be crossed—
and demands the backpack without more ceremony
than when he ties on his coveralls
and unshrouds this morning's corpses.

He cuts first along a withered flank.
The flesh falls, becoming meat,
the last incantation from three hammers
pounding *tsampa* into bones and all,
the meal on which it fed daily with its fellows.

He glances upward to its future—
his face blinding as a single dandelion on a summit—
upward to the first vulture
tentative near ridgetop cairns.

Like the headed club that once simplified encounters,
the remaining spine with skull dangles;
then the skull is crushed, emptied,
something from inside presented.

The men retreat toward sweet, smoldering juniper,
call down the sky to gorge, belch, lounge—
struggle to rise to fledglings ravenous, waiting.
The heart, not acclimated to these specializing furies,
clicks in the roof of the mouth.

(Tibet, 1986)

Little Anodynes

Whenever this pine appears to me,
I might yet become that dawn light on its trunk,

the seasons in its needles that apply
each day as acupuncture and voodoo.

I might yet accompany the blue freighted with clouds
as only evergreen can in stillness

and learn the messages, if any, coded in crows.
Dread may not then press its thumb behind my knee,

nor snowdrifts heap onto nearly-forgotten drifts,
grays defied with a cologned cheek.

The ache in white water honing a canyon night
may no longer approximate my portion of longing.

I am indulged, as if all my friends could gather.
Seduced, as if death kept our promises.

This pine and I stand, neither worthy of the other,
and the stirrings of the shade

remind me of the vertigo
from rising too quickly to our own height.

ONUS

I waited with other men
for a turn in one of the video booths,
pleasure moans surrounding us,
piped over twenty channels.
Made obvious by our desires,
we didn't stand in a line,
didn't look at one another
but with locker room glances.
It's tempting to think we were all lonely,
that we didn't know better
than this questionable connection
to the organized underworld.
Anonymity and acts
without repercussions for me—
that's the play I sought,
though the pros and amateurs
filling the screen with technique
kept becoming people
curiously bruised and scarred,
delighted or bored. Driving away,
I remembered my father
stuck behind a teenage couple
slowing during their kisses
on a two-lane highway,
his horn-honking and curses,
his glare in the rear-view mirror
after we finally raced by.
I thought of my brother
in those months after he came out,
showing off to me
by nodding toward a waiter,
"There's a brother."
I thought of the good man
he now lives with,

who taught him to care;
and of the laughter of a woman
to whose bed I'd returned nude,
holding a dustpan of dog turds and a broom,
announcing, "I am not a demon lover."
I took the usual route,
all of it protection
against, and of, well-being—
like writing these lines to you, love.
Despite the history of tones
predictable afterward,
among the tenderly expendable,
here again is my destination:
your arms held out
with their knowledge and conditions,
which each of us has
every right to want.

A Peel

Yanking off my shirt and ripping it in two for you
was one of those things I do, truly, once.
It surprised me before I could make it into more of a sacrifice.
As you tore the remnants calmly into eighteen pieces,
balled them into a Ziploc, and I labeled it *May 18,*
we proved lovers can be proud—and uncertain—of anything.
I'd almost forgotten that the shirt once belonged
to the hated father of a lover I lived with hopelessly
and that many, like you, have admired the shirt's print,
each time I've worn it—in and out of style—
a discovery of how fast we belong to other lives.
I tell you this now, thinking of that Frenchman
you met on a train at nineteen, who looked at you
unwilling to leave his bed for two weeks
like a sudden, fragrant downpour that should have already ended.
We are older than he and you then put together
with no common language except patience and obssession.
This morning, walking the trashbag to the alley,
I found a hollowed orange under ripening boughs—
remains of the fruit rat's feast. Its color lit the yard,
declared "Don't die hoarding plenty . . ." Inside,
May 18 gazed securely from among our trophies.
I threw it out. Forgive me. I will throw it out again.

THE OLD MENTOR'S REPLY

So, now that you have declined
the grand post in the capitol,
have withdrawn at the last moment
from the favorable marriage
(choosing freedom before power),
you confess to a new, disturbing restlessness:
dreams of banquets, eminent acquaintance,
the dowry of a woman's wit . . .
And the local flora suddenly seem somnolent?
And the town fountains childish?
Until now, your deprivations
were routine, your victories desultory.
Don't confuse ascetic with aesthetic.
Think of Solitude, that sure-footed,
twin-headed creature—man and ass—
rising from the great canyon at evening,
how many days having flowed through the pan,
and it ready to weigh the take,
if any? Think of the small sack of greed,
the heavy dream dust
sprinkled over bedchamber and podium,
and the cup knocking, echoless,
against its bucket. Sleep on that edge,
near the river no bird dares
fly across. Then come to me and complain.

Underprivileged

I'm like the conscience of the boy
who's dropped his half-eaten licorice
in the melee of children leaving
the arranged night at the Y pool.
What can I think as he pretends
to throw it in the trash,
whirls and dodges off, snarfing it
like a spy protecting secrets?
Did I mention he is black and I,
I am white and balding,
and only one of the male volunteers
he tormented in his quest
to be grappled and dunked in affectionate revenge?
It shouldn't matter, should it?
He hasn't noticed me watching,
and the invisible dirt in my mind
differs from his wanting
and not wanting attention.
How did he become my conscience?
Did I mention I am childless,
and the future is not the salve it was
for my self-promoting disappointments?
Briefly, in the shallow end,
he and I spiked a clear beach ball,
dived and volleyed, admiring
with fingertip control
all the happy possibilities
of an understanding aloft between us.
One day—not in my strained, complying arms,
laughing and begging for mercy—
he may rise bitterly into manhood.
He may hate the hard fools we are.
And maybe the fallen sweetness
he salvaged for himself—for me—
will free us from our endless forgiving.

THE BOY WHO WOULD GO NO LOWER IN PRICE

He put away the red woolen poncho
patterned with reindeer among snowflakes,
dialed up his radio's guitar attack
and let my final offer stand beside me
like a freak the street tries not to stare at.

In a town that would hawk its picturesque squalor,
this seemed a practiced closing tactic.
I capitulated, offered more
to grow nicely visible again and gain
the camaraderie in being bested.

He turned away and beggared me,
could afford this pride, perhaps, the power
to withhold, to say No, useless
and pervasive as kitschy souvenirs—
unless it was a way of saying Yes

to disobedience before the larger bargains
at borders bringing out the least in us.
Which is how I choose to see him,
trying, still, to get some purchase
on what we thought each other stood for.

He looked toward lettuce stacked up
like the leafy heads of revolutions,
the tune between us once a hit up North.
I turned toward home and the simpler having,
typically ignorant, tagged after by the cost.

(Nogales, Mexico, 1980)

POSTE RESTANTE: A LETTER FROM DES MOINES TO KATMANDU

Dear Brother,
　　I can see you
in front of that last half sandwich
grinning on the plate, taunting you to finish it
and this making you lonelier.
I can see the umbrella vendor's smug glance
when you refused his bottom offer.
He knew you and the rainy season better, I think,
than you knew either
(not to mention him).
And now I can see you and I are equal
in that mutual ignorance
of having grown up together.
I'd say we have a lot to misunderstand.
　　Why do you assume
that you report from the life I want?
There you wait for a little sunshine
before going off to see some goddess—
who might show herself
if the price is right.
Quite exotic.
I envy you even the loneliness.
But the envy is enough.
　　Today, we dismantled the chain link fence
surrounding "the high-grass prairie education project"
planted last year in the schoolyard.
　　Before mowing,
we pawed through the eye-level growth for debris.
We looked like we were searching for the child fallen
from those 19th-century wagons going West,
the child who comes to
and cries out
and is heard, maybe.

We found two unopened cans of beer.
They were like charms for First Curiosity,
reminders that clouds sometimes pass
like endless migrating buffalo
we would follow
if we knew how or where to.
We stood there
with our hands and blades blackened
by rich, glaciated soil,
by the hope of returning things
to their former, proper size,
and it was not a matter to speak of,
not there at least.
What I mean is
that I can stand here,
in our home town, in the wilderness
of the supermarket's artful packaging,
between the manager's two-way mirror
and the passions like teenage shoplifters,
and I can feel the cashier's long, red nails
as she tries not to touch me
when giving change.
I can know by this
that our local landscape
is not so flat as it might seem
to those flying over, driving through, escaping.
Despite its monocultures, and abandoned barns
you could force poetic wind through,
its revelations
are minute and common
and true enough.
I've made a love from my disaffections,
the undemonstrative kind. Remember how

we slept on horsehides in the summerhouse
and once kept hermit crabs in a porcelain pan?
    You leave this place now
wherever you leave,
and I keep my going by remaining here.
And in that circumstance
lies all the worship
of a goddess,
all the mystery
in a brother who's decided to marry.
    When you get these lines
(if you do), reply soon
and help me understand us.

STEWARDESS

She sits stately by the unlit swimming pool,
all that flesh covered by an orchid-print kaftan
and the sky, a tummy tuck
that must be refused.
Sweet with scotch, she sweeps
her cigarette ash into the water, and Maui
again falls away from her wingtip.
Maui, where she was to be one of those women
who look great for their age. Somehow,
they're all her old girlfriends, still working
night flights, lithe as a single valise
among stars stretched out like endless tennis clubs.
It's not their voices she hears, but the distant
clink of glasses, a salute, a beginning of ease
become a warning bell in villages
near a lava flow. Tonight, her daughters have gone
out with her beauty, three Hawaiian maids
whose help was once inexpensive.
Plumeria—that is what she smells like now.
Let the husbands bribe and flirt, she will not
serve. She toes the water,
cast again into the boiling maw.

ICHETUCKNEE

Prone on the rented inner tube,
we peer through surface reflections,
ours among them mussed by breath. However quiet,
we're too loud for the slow, clear stream
combing water weeds flecked with snails,
each bream and darter—in the deeper, sandy gullies—
holding itself according to the tow. We flow languidly
past the grip of lichen, the nets of sheen wavering like electric current
along mossed ledges and leaf canopies.
Different hunters now, we can ask the ranger about those eggs
like paste pearls clustered on a reed.
We can point to where the fish leaped, twice,
anticipating a third. We've come to grasp a low branch
and hang on, remembering before ourselves,
feeling the huge mouth draw,
and our speculations burn to nothing
on the turtle sun.

BEJEWELED

Dawn warms the rusting toy trucks parked on Lisa's windowsill.
Her cat swats a ping pong ball too still from last night.
I hear the whistling next door, and suddenly it's coming from me,
not really much of a tune on my part. Am I in love?
I whistle to Lisa that I am, though she's gone out
to get us sweet rolls and the Sunday *Times*.
We're canoeing today. We're healthy and pious about canoeing.
The sun will require sun block of us. The clouds will be water and light,
the current water and light, though exquisitely different. There will be a moment
among the green strategies for survival—there always is—
with no faint drone of airplane, no distant highway hiss or shotgun practice.
It's worth the twenty-four-dollar rental fee. It's worth cashing in a Saturday night
early, rising and driving past the stinking paper mill and the retirement town.
It's all ahead of us, like our love, though we've been there before.
Those trucks, for instance, belonged to her father who played
Word Association with her for hours.
And that cat. How she talks to it! Ridiculous!
Except when she strokes me with our private lingo.
I wonder where the whistler next door is headed.
Gems of water from the shower glisten on my shoulders,
that itch I refuse now to wipe away.

FIVE PRIVACIES

As he rows,
she opens her blouse
for the sun.

. . .

They hold each other
so close, they
each see a horizon.

. . .

Reading all her books to know her better,
he turns the page and notices
her reading over his shoulder.

. . .

For the first time, she awakens to his stare.

. . .

She upstairs,
he downstairs,
they rise from their work
at the same sound.

They watch from windows.
Two geese keep swimming,
stirring their small pool
in the middle
of the frozen pond.

PROFILE

Converging at the corner of the eye,
lines, faint and deep, suggest a point to sight:
time gathering at that periphery
wholly individual yet not quite—
because I look on you and you on me
secretly (or with the vain permission
in the other's feigning sleep or study),
desiring to see beyond possession.
But those lines diverge, too—an argument
against the single focus, experience
fanning out its wrinkles in a dumb show.
So our two-faced love seems doubly intent,
presenting, as its oblique evidence,
the side we view, the other we might know.

Interview with Echo

There was your bed
with him in it.

There was the unbolted screen
and the window he'd come through

with fresh-cut roses.
Roses, for chrissakes!

Poor boy . . . gorgeous
and expert, but not *him.*

How many nights lay
in both of you like this?—

the sympathetic tongue
on the stricken nipple,

the nerve crying
"So this is how we die?"

And *him?* Drowned
embracing a reflection—

yet reclining by the pond
in your dreams, the calm there

begging for the push
and the thrashing below.

And after the suitor left
embarrassed, bewildered,

you gave the roses
to your neighbor again,

who gave them to another
as his own.

Now you're off the subject.
Or are you?

You who repeat yourself
in different ways.

A Better Muse

I remember her voice
the night the best man turned toward her
as he slipped off his shorts
and dived from the floating dock;
Isn't that like men,
she muttered to me, bitterly.
I thought she meant
Isn't that like <u>you</u>.

I was easily accused,
young with old anger,
and she wore her one dress
as a favor to the bride,
from some part of our closet
I'd never seen.
It puckered and revealed
an awkwardness
I dared not tell her
I found beautiful.
Too confining, she'd said,
though her usual jeans fit
like water to a fin.

She must have hated that dress
to slip out of it
for the darkness
the best man and the wedding party treaded,
darkness that transports a voice
too far. She took it with her
when she left me
for a better muse,
and, in dreams, I dived into it,
hoping to drown.

Across the years, she tells me
to leave her sorrow
alone. She says those tears
my fists grind
back into my eyes—
tears too mortal and ancient
to be mine—
are mine
when they come.

I resist her as I listen.
It's our wont,
trying to be known.
Because of it, I want tonight—
you and I here
in this house naked
beneath its paint,
choosing what words will
enter and stay.

Betrothal Park: Iowa

They sloshed across this bend,
she blinded by gunpowder,
he yanking her through brambles
up the bank to the Wheeler place.
They had escaped ambush before.
Once that summer, Springfield Trust
was empty when they entered.
A teller cocked his pistol
as they fired on the cages.

Their current still flows here—
though the park, sold later
during the war, is stumps
and the opulence of a cow's eye.
You could look all day. No more
honeymoon cabins. No plaques.
Wheeler's Ford coupe shines
in the basement of the county museum,
95 holes still rifled for fingers
fifty years after those kids tried
to hot-wire their way across the state line.

An old widow tells it now
if you call on Saturday morning:
Prohibition, Great Depression,
drought dust gathering on wedding gowns
before you could say *I do.*
Every couple here that day but one
had children when fields prospered.
Some own lots on the reservoir nearby.
Did they hear their bird calling, that dawn
when the posse whistled behind those trees?
Oak to jack pine: Wake the two
most wanted.

For the Holidays

My sister and I roam a stand of pine
unloaded in the parking lot at Sears.
Each tree, even the scrawniest and most overpriced,
is wired for upright display
to a cross of lath.
I decline their symbolic possibilities,
giving up books for the day.
And I also refuse to imagine us lost together,
bucked by an uncle's roan
who knew the big woods and the way to the barn—
though I'm fool enough at times
to wish us a past like that.
We've been shopping through crowds all day,
and not one familiar face.
Now she wants the largest tree
that will fit her apartment.
I can't judge our dimensions.
Under strings of star-shaped lights,
she has the haggard beauty of a young woman
late for work,
secretly proud of making love too far into night.
It is almost as if she has not had a child
to escape her father,
and another to keep a husband long gone.
It is almost as if I have never found a book
to look into when the shouting started.
It is almost that simple,
she is so beautiful,
unwiring our choice from one of the crosses.

A CANDLE

May I . . . show an affirming flame.
                    —W. H. Auden, *"September 1, 1939"*

I turn a corner at empty streets and find a candle in a red cup
no larger than a whiskey glass.
In the breeze the flame wavers, rattles faintly and remains.
The killed above it on the plaque on the ramshackle wall
have not been dead long enough.
Those, like me, with no relatives here,
no bond here except breath,
have not discovered this corner enough.
I think of the wall-painting of the moonlit cruiseship
in the collaborators' barracks at Auschwitz—
its will to diversion—
and wonder if that place will last, say, as long as the Pyramids.
I stand and think of the round table
at which, tonight, the Occupiers cede power.
The future is coming here again—
change like the trolley
that halves the passed-out drunk on its tracks.
The apple trees bloom against gray facades.
The years of purgatorial talk in Cafe Perseverance
were useful somehow.
In the small glow, I think of Anya down the block,
thirteen and shouting *No!* at her shouting father.
Anya and her friends under a streetlight in spring.
The rivers flow with filings denied, officially, until now,
and children will return with their fifty years in exile.
Beside the candle lies the obligatory rose,
freshly cut by the old meanings. I lift it
and feel its coolness,
and its flame that can't be held
enough.

(Lodz, Poland, 1989)

76

FATHER AND SON AND

They've lived long enough
to find this manmade lake,
to let the moon sink now
like a dominating grudge
and allow the stars
their larger, shifting patterns.

With a lantern, a frayed net
discovered in the toolshed,
a rod with reel snarled
by the grandchildren's outing,
they work the time made perfect
because it's available,
their readiness a dug-up bait
hooked from within.

At the ends of their hindered casts,
it wriggles above drowned trees,
anchoring the moment
like the dream house
built behind them
on an incline toward the water.

Beneath them, the dock
in need of straightening
against the yearly floe—
the dock for the boat someday—
stands with their stillness,
quivers with their blundering,
no catch too small to keep.

So their forbearance, their grace
has some alcohol on its breath,
a few stories, an answer

they hadn't thought to ask for;
and they're expected home.

They'll stay the one night here
reconciled, their haul—
left on a stringer pegged
to fifty feet of paid-for shoreline—
devoured while they sleep.

LAST PHOTOGRAPH OF HIS BACHELOR HAND

In his open left palm, a blackbird stands
minutes after it attacked its reflection,
a window as flat as its eye and harder.
Dazed still, it sways on splayed talons
while his palm dips and lifts slightly.
Go on, he says to its leaden lightness,
urging the sky to resume its lost height.
Once, when he was single of mind,
he could ignore such troubling gravity,
this beak that gapes as if trying to explain
or ask, *What happened?* More able now
are the lurking cat and worm below
to tear their piece from unflappable wings.
Less willing is he to let this world drop
without a thought as, perhaps, it should.
When did he promise himself such faithfulness?
Before him, his fiancée focuses and snaps.
In the feathers at the back of the gleaming head,
a faint rainbow mirrors his own collisions:
the blinding punch delivered to the self
enraged at its failings, greedy with its fear;
the shock of recognition—colors in blackness—
that separates a man from his flight.
Too much, he thinks, to see in this bird, and too little,
on this day before his marriage vows.
Go on, he says to ambiguous life
as it hops, woozy, to the berry bush,
and he looks at his hand, ringless yet changed,
his love presenting him the evidence.

TRAVELS OF RUSTICIANO OF PISA

Upon returning to Italy from decades of wandering, Marco Polo became embroiled in civil war and was imprisoned for three years. During this time, he met Rusticiano, a minor literary man, who then acted, officially, as his amanuensis in the composition of the book that spurred the European imagination and immortalized him.

Prison is hard for a man who hasn't sat.
Polo boasted that the Great Khan had detained him
with years of entertainments and diplomatic duties,
so indispensable he'd grown, as well as homesick.
His secret heart fancied a book in this.
I had him dictating in minutes—to pass my time.
Boredom, however, or suspicion soon silenced him,
and I couldn't leave him alone. Life is stitched with journeys
snapped, reknotted as one can; unspun thread lay in him.
How I questioned, cajoled, damned . . . begged!
playing the faithful wife in husbanding
his store of trifles delivered profoundly.
Awakened past midnight, I saved those worth my shorthand.
And sometimes, at climactic turns, he faltered
as if lost in a lie . . . but the denouements I offered
and he praised as "telepathy, nothing less"
now seem pieces won in a game larger than coauthorship:
my visions of places he recalled too well to recount,
too much done and undone, perhaps—
a life not quite new nor his.
I loved this torture in him, and this play—
and his voice at twilight unafraid of itself alone,
discoursing in tongues I couldn't understand,
a rich nothingness sent, I'll wager, to one far away.
When he was ransomed, I felt as he that morning
a crow stole his last pearl while he bathed,
the Levantine desert silenced by the thief's mouthful.
How many fortunes we'd made together and lost!

Some know it is easier to be saintly or wicked than truthful
and judge our *Description of the World* fool's facts.
Can we know what digression forgets and decorum excises?
Its success attests to their craving for gossip,
landscapes ill-mapped and lands merely reopened.
I haven't seen Polo since our parting, and it's best.
The conjugal knot preoccupies his thread now.
I wish to think he's soothed.
For how many princesses need one deliver?
How many of the Buddha's teeth need one purchase
before he must do something else with his spirit
like fire that has cleaned asbestos capes?
I lingered over these glories as over ashes.
Now I ransom myself in first person.

DELICATE ARCH

Tell me what pose is most natural
for us so small under this vault of rock.
I touched where I could reach,
where it sweated far below its thinnest place,
and I turned:
                 across the huge, wind-pocked bowl,
behind Dick and Shirley and the lens,
vapor trails crossed from flights east-west;
birds circled to roost on a ridge of piñon pine.

That's why I gathered the litter for this snapshot—
to be larger.
          That's why I'm waving
as the arch reddens and our faces flush dusky at last,
my one hand wet with stone,
the other clutching fire
                 we will speak across in camp.

(Arches National Park, Utah, 1979)

The Fireplace

—for Paul Aschim, Russ Berndt, and John Schroeder

Late in the mountain cabin, the low flame
on the thick logs' sheath of coals
leaps and pops and dwindles with our talk
to a single wavering scrim, focusing the soul
of the rented place we've shared for three days
on a point of friendship, love, and world.
The scrim splits into a pair of minute figures,
vaguely human, dancing round each other
as in a festival of almost touching,
some sacrifice to soothe the gods perhaps,
or wean each mind from its solitary fate.
The pair vaults suddenly, embracing
for a moment, amorous, or rapacious—
wrestlers practicing technique,
a parent holding all the crying in the child.
They meld, nearly indistinguishable.
And just as suddenly from within, a blow
hurls them apart, into several new beings
public, collegial, obliged, failing.
Across the white ash of their stage,
they group and smash, retreat and trade places,
eliminate and save each other or themselves
temporarily. We watch these variations on our lives,
the hearth, capacious and comprehensible,
containing them more snugly than the heart.
We need not turn our faces lit by history
toward each other or ourselves.
Friends tell a story to their flickering darkness.
That's partly why we've come together
so far from other bonds beyond the mountain,
to listen and see what more there is to burning.